HOPE FOR THE HURTING

BY

BEVERLY L. BUCKINGHAM
Steele

PHOTOGRAPHY BY TRAVIS WHITMAN

INFINITY
PUBLISHING

All rights reserved. No part of this book shall be reproduced or transmitted in any form or by any means, electronic, mechanical, magnetic, photographic including photocopying, recording or by any information storage and retrieval system, without prior written permission of the publisher. No patent liability is assumed with respect to the use of the information contained herein. Although every precaution has been taken in the preparation of this book, the publisher and author assume no responsibility for errors or omissions. Neither is any liability assumed for damages resulting from the use of the information contained herein.

Copyright © 2010 by Beverly L. Buckingham

All Scripture quotations, unless otherwise indicated, are taken from the Holy Bible: New International Version, NIV (emphasis mine).

ISBN 0-7414-5987-6

Printed in the United States of America

Published July 2010

INFINITY PUBLISHING
1094 New DeHaven Street, Suite 100
West Conshohocken, PA 19428-2713
Toll-free (877) BUY BOOK
Local Phone (610) 941-9999
Fax (610) 941-9959
Info@buybooksontheweb.com
www.buybooksontheweb.com

TABLE of CONTENTS

PREFACE 1

JESUS, SON OF GOD

HIS NAME IS JESUS: POEM 6
JESUS GIVES A WARNING 7
JESUS IS GOING AWAY 8
JESUS WELCOMES OUR QUESTIONS 9
JESUS REVEALS TRUTH 10
JESUS INVITES US TO PRAY 11
JESUS WILL RETURN TO THE FATHER 12
JESUS HAS OVERCOME THE WORLD 13
CHRIST CAME IN: POEM 14
RICHES IN JESUS: POEM 15

IN OUR GRIEF

WHEN LOSS OVERWHELMS ME: POEM 18
WHEN GRIEF ARRIVES 19
GRIEF AND SHOCK 20
STRUGGLING WITH GRIEF 21
FACING DEPRESSION IN GRIEF 22
GRIEF'S CRY 23
LETTING GO OF GRIEF 24
GRIEF'S OUTCOME 25
IN MY GRIEF: POEM 26
GOD'S GRACE FOR MY LOSS: POEM 27

IN OUR LONELINESS

FACING LONELINESS: POEM 30
LONELINESS 31
LONELINESS FOR THE APOSTLE PAUL 32
ETERNAL CONFIDENCE IN LONELY TIMES 33
OUR INITIATIVE IN LONELY TIMES 34
THE LORD STANDS WITH US IN LONELY TIMES 35
THE LORD STRENGTHENS US IN LONELY TIMES 36
THE LORD USES US IN LONELY TIMES 37
FRIENDS: POEM 38
THE LORD IN YOUR MIDST: POEM 39

THE HANDS OF GOD

IN HIS HANDS: POEM 42
OUR HANDS—GOD'S HANDS 43
GOD'S NAIL-SCARRED HANDS 44
GOD'S HANDS ARE SECURE 45
GOD'S HAND OF DISCIPLINE 46
OUR TIMES ARE IN GOD'S HANDS 47
GOD'S VICTORIOUS HAND 48
OUR LIVES IN GOD'S HANDS 49
GOD'S COMFORT TO OUR SOUL: POEM 50
LOVING-KINDNESS: POEM 51

IN TROUBLED TIMES

TROUBLES TURN TO REST: POEM 54
TROUBLE ON EVERY SIDE 55
SEEKING GOD IN TROUBLED TIMES 56
DO NOT BE AFRAID 57
TAKE UP YOUR POSITION 58
STAND FIRM 59
PRAISE AND FAITH 60
REST ON EVERY SIDE 61
WHEN TROUBLES COME: POEM 62
VICTORY IN THE STORM: POEM 63
HOW CAN I KNOW HIM? 64

PREFACE

"Blessed is the man whose strength is in you, whose heart is set on pilgrimage, as they pass through the Valley of Baca, they make it a spring; the rain also covers it with pools. They go from strength to strength; every one of them appears before God in Zion" (Psalms 84:5–7 NKJ).

Have you ever noticed how often we try to work things out on our own or according to what the world offers as solutions? I have, especially as we pass through the valley of Baca—the valley of weeping.

Valleys of weeping will be different for each of us, but we all pass through them. Sometimes it's an unexpected illness, financial difficulties, or the loss of someone dear to us. For others, it may be conflict between family members, living with someone who has an addiction, or dealing with the stress of unemployment.

The good news is that God says we can be blessed—having joy in all things, when we find our strength and help in Him, instead of in ourselves or in worldly ways. How can this happen? Does this passage of Scripture give us any clues?

First of all, our heart needs to be set on completing the journey with our Lord even when we face tough times. God's Word says: *"As they pass through the valley of Baca they make it a spring . . ." (verse 6a).* Making our troubles a spring means we learn to rejoice through our trials and sing through our tears. We discover the blessings of hope and healing in the very places that threaten to destroy us.

The secret in doing the above is found in verse 6b: *"the rain also covers it with pools."* Rain in Scripture is often used as a symbol of the Holy Spirit, and water as the Word of God. Jesus said, in John 7:38 NKJ: *"He who believes in me, as Scripture has said, 'out of his heart will flow rivers of living water.'"* The Holy Spirit, along with the Word of God, brings rest and refreshment for weary travelers in the valley of weeping. They also make us aware of our need to repent, reconcile, and be restored.

The Spirit's ministry of refreshment may touch our lives through a card, phone call, visit, flowers, meals, prayers, etc. Recently while I was in my own valley of Baca, God touched me through a phone call. Someone I shared Christ with, years before, wanted to thank me by taking me out to breakfast.

We, too, will go from strength to strength [increase in victorious power] as our journey continues. Our trials will make us stronger, as we look for God's blessings in the valley of Baca. He wants to turn our hard places into a platform for His glory, and then one day, when our pilgrimage ends, we will see our King in all His beauty.

Beverly Buckingham

DEDICATION

I dedicate my book, *Hope for the Hurting,* to my longtime friend and prayer partner, Betty Ditmer. Her prayers and constant encouragement concerning my writing have played a large part in this book being completed.

JESUS, SON OF GOD

OUR LIVING WATER

HIS NAME IS JESUS

There is one to whom we go,
When our hearts are feeling low;
He comforts us just then,
On this we can depend.
His name is Jesus.

When the soul in anguish cries,
Until tears fill up our eyes;
There is one who loves and cares;
There is one who answers prayers.
His name is Jesus.

If our body's filled with pain,
His mighty touch is just the same.
His hand alone holds power to heal;
He understands just how we feel.
His name is Jesus.

In time of sorrow or in grief,
He brings to us sweet relief.
It matters not how oft' we plead;
He fulfills our every need.
His name is Jesus.

Praise God for this one who shares,
Each burden we are called to bear.
Never has there been such love,
As God's own Son, sent from above.
His name is Jesus.

"And my God will meet all your needs according to His glorious riches in Christ Jesus."
(Philippians 4:19)

JESUS GIVES A WARNING

Bible Reading: John 16:1–4

Jesus, knowing He will soon be leaving the disciples, wants His disciples to be aware of what they will face without His physical presence.

"They will put you out of the synagogue; in fact, a time is coming when anyone who kills you will think he is offering a service to God" (v. 2). He warns His disciples so they will not go astray when they are persecuted because of their faith in Him. We don't know how much the disciples understood at that moment, but Jesus knew that one day they would see clearly. In John 15:18, Jesus says: *"If the world hates you, keep in mind that it hated me first. If you belonged to the world, it would love you as its own. As it is, you do not belong to the world, but I have chosen you out of the world. That is why the world hates you."*

We admire Christians worldwide who stand up for Jesus, regardless of the hostility and harassment they face daily. What about us? Do the people we work with know we love God? Do we speak up for truth and righteousness when we have the opportunity? Do we turn away from gossip and evil talk? Jesus loved His disciples enough to warn them that it would not be easy to follow Him. He also promised them He would send the Counselor, the Spirit of truth, to be with them forever (John 14:15–17). Let's heed His warning and run with His promise!

Prayer: Lord Jesus, teach me to regard your warnings, and rely upon your promises.

JESUS IS GOING AWAY

Bible Reading: John 16:5–16

Have you ever wondered how Jesus' disciples felt as their dreams were shattered? They were expecting Jesus to set up His kingdom on earth, and suddenly He's talking about going away. *"Now I am going to Him who sent me, yet none of you asks me, 'Where are you going?' Because I have said these things, you are filled with grief" (vv. 5, 6).*

Our dreams can change abruptly too. We receive news our child will never walk again. Our spouse dies without warning. We become the victim of stolen identity. Our lives, like the disciples', are plunged into a new direction that makes no sense at all.

Jesus understands the disciples' grief, but He wants them to look beyond it. His mission on earth is nearly complete; His going away has a purpose. *"But I tell you the truth: It is for your good that I am going away. Unless I go away, the Counselor will not come to you; but if I go, I will send Him to you" (v. 7). ". . . He will guide you into all truth" (v. 13).*

Will we allow God to help us work through our pain and grief? Will we look beyond today, and find His purpose for our remaining years? Psalms 31:14, 15 speaks to our need: *"But I trust in you, O Lord; I say, 'You are my God.' My times are in your hands."*

Prayer: Father, help me release my shattered dreams to you, and to embrace your purpose for my life.

JESUS WELCOMES OUR QUESTIONS

Bible Reading: John 16:16–21

Jesus makes a profound statement in verse 16: *"In a little while you will see me no more, and then after a little while you will see me."* The puzzled disciples mumble questions among themselves. *"What does He mean by 'a little while'? We don't understand what He is saying" (v. 18).* Jesus was not surprised at the disciples' confusion. He knew what they desired to ask Him, and tells them so: *". . . Are you asking one another what I meant?" (v. 19).*

Do Jesus' words ever baffle you? They baffle me sometimes. Recently, I thought God was asking me to take on an unthinkable task. "Is this really you, God?" I queried. I wondered: Where will I find the time? Will I follow through on a commitment like this? God addressed my questions through His Word at our annual missionary conference. The answers were so clear it seemed the speaker had heard me ask the questions. Jesus' personal interest uplifted me. As godly counsel and circumstances affirmed the Word of God, I moved ahead by faith.

Jesus received the disciples' questions with gladness. He wanted them to envision the coming joy no one could take away from them (vv. 20, 21). He understands our questions, too. He wants them to mature us, deepen our relationship with Him. Are there questions on your heart today? Jesus welcomes our questions.

Prayer: Almighty God, help me to ask you all my questions, and patiently wait for your response.

JESUS REVEALS TRUTH

Bible Reading: John 16:20–24

We can always count on Jesus to reveal the truth about our circumstances. He may not tell us everything, but what we do hear we can depend on and it will be sufficient. Take for instance the words He spoke to His disciples when He was about to enter His last days on earth. He knew they didn't understand His figurative language, so He explained it to them in verses 20 through 22.

Jesus speaks candidly about the difficult time the disciples will face as He endures the Cross. The world will rejoice because it thinks it is getting rid of Jesus, but the disciples, who love Him, will weep and mourn over His death and burial. They left all to follow Jesus. They must have wondered how this could be happening.

What difficult place are you up against in your life? I recall the inner struggle I had for two years beginning in 1995. Two of our children were facing unwanted divorces. In the midst of this pain my husband died. These were dark and stressful days, but Jesus wanted me, like the disciples, to know the truth. He understands our grief. Our joy may be hidden momentarily, but it will break through again. He told His disciples their grief would turn to joy. He wants us to receive the same message. When we know Jesus, nothing can take away our deep joy in Him. This is His promise in verse 22, and Jesus can be trusted to reveal the truth. He is the Truth!

Prayer: Lord Jesus, reveal your truth to me as I grieve. I want to work through my pain.

JESUS INVITES US TO PRAY

Bible Reading: John 16:23–27

Have you ever prayed for something and been amazed at God's answer? One summer morning I was headed to the lake to spend time with my son's family. "Help me to be a good witness for you, God," I prayed as I drove along. We had an enjoyable afternoon on the lake, but as we were docking the pontoon, my son dropped his van keys into the water. I began to pray that God would show us what to do. A lady with a large magnet came to our rescue, but to no avail.

My son hurried off to call a locksmith while ten-year-old Andy lounged in the driver's seat. My mind raced with the words, *Try your car keys in the van.* I argued with myself: *How ridiculous.* But the thought persisted until I said, "Andy, I want you to try my keys in the ignition—don't jam them—we don't want them to get stuck." The keys slid in with ease. Andy turned them and, to our amazement, the van started! When my son returned and heard the van running, he threw up his arms and asked, "How in the world did this work?" Pointing upward I said, "Only God!"

"Ask and you will receive," Jesus tells His disciples in verse 24. We find a similar statement in Matthew 7:7: *"Ask and it will be given to you."* What blessings we miss when we limit God or neglect to pray for small things. Let's accept our Savior's invitation to pray in His name. As we do, our faith will grow, and God will be glorified.

Prayer: Enlarge my prayer life, Father. Teach me to come to you for all things—even the small ones.

JESUS WILL RETURN TO THE FATHER

Bible Reading: John 16:28–31

Jesus, the Son of God, who left His place in heaven to be born of a virgin, now, tells His disciples He will leave the world and return to His Father. He knows the hour of His death, burial, and resurrection is near. His work on Earth will soon be complete as He provides a way of salvation for all humankind. His words open up the understanding of the disciples, who proclaim: *"Now you are speaking clearly and without figures of speech. Now we can see that you know all things and that you do not even need to have anyone ask you questions. This makes us believe that you came from God"* (vv. 29–30).

The finished work of Jesus is for the entire world. Do we understand what that means for us personally? Many of us do, but there are still those who do not know. While I served on a short-term mission trip to Costa Rica, one man told me he had no idea why Jesus died on the Cross. I had the wonderful privilege of sharing the "Good News" with him, and he prayed to receive Jesus Christ. A 95-year-old lady put her faith in Jesus while I volunteered at a nursing home. This same Jesus, who told His disciples He would return to the Father, says to us, *"Go into all the world and preach the good news to all creation" (Mark 16:15).* Do you know someone who needs to hear?

Prayer: Thank you, Jesus, for the finished work of Calvary. Use me to tell others the "Good News" about you.

JESUS HAS OVERCOME THE WORLD

Bible Reading: John 16:31–33

Jesus rejoices with the disciples saying, *"You believe at last!" (v. 31)*. He goes on to tell them a time is coming when they will be scattered—going to their own homes. He will be left alone. He explains, *"I have told you these things, so that in me you may have peace" (v. 33)*. Imagine the disciples' puzzled faces at this moment. They may have asked: How can this be? How can He expect us to have peace when we have depended on being with Him? Jesus doesn't allow them to wonder long. He continues to speak. *"In this world you will have trouble. But take heart! I have overcome the world" (v. 33)*.

There are troubles in the lives of believers today too. We work thirty years for one company only to lose our retirement. Our loved ones suffer through radiation treatments, yet die. We are misunderstood because we value life. Families are torn apart by ungodly choices that cause some to stumble. We cry out, "Where can we find peace in the midst of our misery?" Jesus' response has not changed: *"Take heart! I have overcome the world" (v. 33)*.

> When troubles come, as we know they will,
> God has a special plan;
> And though the way is dark for us,
> There's rest within His hand.

Prayer: Father, I want to believe regardless of the troubles in my life. Show me the way.

CHRIST CAME IN

If I could choose a million words
To tell what Christ means to me,
It would not be enough I'm sure,
He means so much, you see.

For once I wandered helplessly
So lost in all my sin,
Praise God that He did seek me out,
And now I've entered in.

For all my sin I could not pay.
He said, "No debt you owe."
This gift was bought at Calvary,
And freely it's bestowed.

I now have access to a throne,
Where boldly I can come.
And tell Him of my heart's desires,
He hears them every one.

Although once I was unworthy,
It can no longer be.
For as my Father looks within,
It's Christ He sees in me.

At last I know I've found a Friend,
Who never will depart.
Could I do less than tell of Him,
Who lives within my heart?

*"Therefore, if anyone is in Christ, he is a new creation;
the old has gone, the new has come!"
(2 Corinthians 5:17)*

RICHES IN JESUS

O Lord I am not wealthy,
Yet I am rich indeed.
I'm finding hidden treasures
Since I believed in Thee.

As I look around this world,
I find no greater thrill,
Than to know my Savior cares,
And keeps me in His will.

Precious is the thought I have,
He watches with His eye.
Whispers in the darkest hour,
"Be not afraid, it's I."

Earthly things may bring me gain,
But never peace within.
What profit would it be for me
To lose my soul in sin?

The flesh is weak, like the grass,
It will but fade away.
His robe of righteousness, my choice
To greet Him in that day.

Then clothed in all His glory,
I'll come before His throne,
Where evermore I'll reign with Christ,
For heaven will be my home.

*"The name of the Lord is a strong tower;
the righteous run to it and are safe."
(Proverbs 18:10)*

IN OUR GRIEF

GOD SENDS LIGHT

WHEN LOSS OVERWHELMS ME

In times when loss overwhelms me,
I long to comprehend;
And yet I know that I cannot,
It's God's to understand.

I only know the pain I have
Is deep and very real;
It hurts so much inside of me,
And touches all I feel.

At times, my body too gives way
Beneath life's crushing blows;
Especially when to human eyes,
The victors are my foes.

And still it's in these hurtful times
My spirit's taught to soar;
I find a refuge in you, Lord,
Like none I've known before.

My loss relinquished to your care
Will lose its powerful sting;
As in my heart you place a song,
And give me strength to sing.

A song of hope, of truth, of love,
That no loss can erase;
For I have found the victory, Lord,
Through your amazing grace.

*"God is our refuge and strength,
An ever-present help in trouble."
(Psalms 46:1)*

WHEN GRIEF ARRIVES

Bible Reading: Genesis 37:1–28

Grief—how often it arrives as an unexpected intruder. And even when we anticipate it, we are never ready for its arrival. Imagine the abrupt change in Joseph's life when an errand to check on his brothers resulted in being stripped of his colorful garment, thrown into a pit, and sold into slavery. The treacherous actions of Joseph's brothers brought grief to both him and his father.

In February 1997, my personal encounter with grief began while conversing with my husband. Suddenly he stretched out his arm, reached toward his back, and blurted out: "Oh, the pain!" In seconds, I was dialing 911. After several hours at a local hospital, I was told he had a thoracic aneurysm and needed to be transported to the Cleveland Clinic. I had no time to prepare for the days ahead. I would need to draw from the "living waters" of my personal relationship with God. I think Joseph had to do the same in his dilemma.

We can count on God to uphold us whenever we experience grief, but it's best to build our relationship with Him daily. Doing so equips us to respond to His grace in life's crises. As we discover more about grief in the devotions ahead, let's begin by making sure our foundation is built on Jesus Christ, the One who can prepare us for grief's arrival.

Prayer: Search my heart, Lord. I want my foundation to endure in times of grief.

GRIEF AND SHOCK

Bible Reading: Genesis 37:29–36

We do not welcome grief in the beginning, for the reality of our hurt seems more than we can bear. Our body usually reacts by going into shock, and many erect a wall of denial. At first, this is a good thing, giving our body and emotions the necessary time to absorb our excruciating pain. Reflecting on Jacob's grief in Scripture, we see a man tearing at his clothes, putting on sackcloth, and mourning many days for his son.

My heart ached following my husband's death in May 1997, but my emotions seemed under control. A surge of energy erupted, allowing me to make legal decisions, have the grandchildren visit, paint, and complete yard work. However, as the leaves began to change color, my real feelings surfaced. It became difficult to pretend I wasn't hurting, and stopping the tears was impossible. At first, I didn't recognize this as grief; I only knew I was weary and frightened.

Jacob's reaction is understandable too. We wouldn't expect him to accept lightly the news about his beloved Joseph. But Jacob becomes stuck in his grief, choosing to live in fear of loss instead of processing his pain. We see this in Genesis 42:4, 36–38.

Shock is our friend for a season, but if we do not face the reality of our loss, we are setting ourselves up for greater emotional pain. Grief must do its work.

Prayer: Father, I feel frightened and insecure. Help me face my real feelings and remember you understand my sorrow.

STRUGGLING WITH GRIEF

Bible Reading: 1 Samuel 1:1–20

As cracks appear in the wall of our denial, our true feelings seep through, and we enter into grief's struggle. Some of us have repressed our emotions for only a short time; others for years, leading to a lifetime of anger and depression. In our Bible reading, we learn Hannah's sorrow has been long term. She yearns for a child. Her husband questions her: *"Hannah, why are you weeping? Why don't you eat? Why are you downhearted?" (v. 8).*

Struggling with grief affects us not only emotionally, but also physically. Hannah is not hungry. Have you ever lost your appetite while grieving? I have. I have also been exhausted yet unable to sleep. In verse 10, we read: *"In bitterness of soul Hannah wept much, and prayed to the Lord."* Hannah was a woman of God with a broken and sorrowful spirit. How often it seems we too will crumble when we are confronted with our genuine feelings. And if we are misunderstood, as Hannah was, the way of grief becomes dark and lonely.

In the depths of my grief, I recall crying out to God and journaling these words: Father, my heart is overwhelmed. I seem unable to stop the racing of my mind. Desperate thoughts threaten to trap me. I feel like I'm losing control. Come to me and quiet me in your presence. Remind me that you are with me. Teach me to rely on you for the unknown path ahead.

Prayer: Lord Jesus, I bring you my broken heart. Hold me and heal me in your way—in your timing.

FACING DEPRESSION IN GRIEF

Bible Reading: Psalms 42

While we travel along the path of grief, our deepest valley is often depression. Surely, the writer of Psalms 42 expresses it adequately. *"My tears have been my food day and night. Why are you downcast, O my soul? Why so disturbed within me? . . . I say to God my Rock, 'Why have you forgotten me?'" (vv. 3a, 5a, 9a)*

I became well acquainted with depression while grieving. At first, I suffered in silence. I felt alone, as though I was groping through a dense fog. Fear held me in a tight grip. I had difficulty suppressing periods of strenuous crying. Feelings of guilt ran deep.

We hear the psalmist crying out, but even in the midst of his despondency, he proclaims that God is his rock—his hope for the future. He is confident God will command His loving-kindness in the daytime and give him a song in the night (vv. 8–11). God can be trusted to do the same for us.

When facing despair we should not give up but call out to God, telling Him exactly how we feel. Jesus is touched by the feelings of our weaknesses. He understands our pain. Read Hebrews 4:14–16. We also need to move through the fear of asking others for help. It's okay to contact a friend, pastor, or counselor. Above all, hope in God. He has a future for all who grieve, even the depressed!

Prayer: Come to me in my despondency, Father—I need you!

GRIEF'S CRY

Bible Reading: Psalms 61

Those in grief have been known to cry out "Why?" or "How long?" a thousand times and receive only silence in return. The pain of grief can be intense and sharp, cutting into the core of our inner being while tearing away any protective covering we have left. And once our anger, guilt, fears, and loneliness are exposed, we, like the psalmist, call out: *"Hear my cry, O God; listen to my prayer. . . I call as my heart grows faint; lead me to the rock that is higher than I" (vv. 1, 2).*

This was the cry of my heart in March 1998 when I attended an all-day concert called "Daughters of Promise." Depressed and with questions racing through my mind, I was out of touch with my feelings. Strangely, I don't remember one thing said that day, but I do recall being bathed in the awesome love of God. As His love flowed over me, my wounded heart caught a glimpse of the light at the end of the journey, and my emotional baggage opened. In the weeks that followed, I began to work through the emotions that held my spirit captive.

Our grief cannot separate us from God's love—nothing can! Read Romans 8:28–39. When our heart cries out in pain, God listens. He cares! Let's take time to be alone with Him even when we are hurting. His open arms await our coming!

Prayer: Thank you, Lord, for your unfailing love. Hear my cry as I wait upon you today.

LETTING GO OF GRIEF

Bible Reading: Ecclesiastes 3:1–11

We should not allow anyone to rob us of our grief. It's important to face our loss and experience our heartache fully. Grief comes with no set time; each person and situation is unique. The writer of Ecclesiastes says, *"There is a time for everything, and a season for every activity under heaven" (v. 1).* His words encourage us: there is a time to weep and mourn—a time to heal and laugh again.

Letting go of grief is not easy, but it is a reality we can all experience. I found it helpful to write letters to my deceased husband. I told him what I was thinking and feeling, kept him informed about our family and church. At first, I wrote several letters a week, but in time, the task became burdensome. God used His Word and my continued journaling to bring me into the complete realization that my husband had departed to a better place. I still had my life to live. I was at a juncture that necessitated asking myself some questions: What will I keep alive from our relationship? What will I let go of? In the fall of 2000, I wrote my final goodbye letter.

Saying goodbye does not mean we forget that loved one. There will always be special occasions and memories that trigger deep emotions, but saying goodbye does indicate we are letting go of grief. We are ready to move on with life.

Prayer: Father, you have given me the courage to grieve. Grant me your strength to let go and your wisdom to move on with my life.

GRIEF'S OUTCOME

Bible Reading: 2 Corinthians 1:3–11

As our journey through grief nears completion, we begin to talk about the future with hope again. We dare to think our lives can be rebuilt. There's a fresh longing to help another traveler along the way.

The outcome of our grief will be expressed and experienced both inwardly and outwardly.

Inwardly, we discover "treasures in darkness"—security in the storm, strength made perfect in weakness, sufficient light for our next step. Outwardly, we want to produce fruit from our pain that will help and comfort others.

As I continued to heal, God amazed me by opening a door to serve at our local hospital as a volunteer assistant chaplain. I often found myself at the bedside of a widow. The long hours I spent with her became productive in finishing a poem booklet titled *For Those Who Suffer*. In the fall of 2000, I had my first experience in facilitating a support group for those who were recovering from the losses of life.

Whenever we allow, God will bring significance and purpose out of our grief. *"And we know that in all things God works for the good of those who love Him, who have been called according to His purpose" (Romans 8:28).* He does not say "all things are good," but "that in all things God works for good." This includes grief's outcome.

Prayer: Lead me on, Father, in the ways you know will enlarge my heart. Produce fruit from my pain.

IN MY GRIEF

Here I am Lord in my grief,
From my sorrow to seek relief;
I can't express the hurt I feel;
I only know that it is real.

It shakes my very soul within
Until my mind begins to spin;
And in my helplessness I cry,
"Why did this loved one have to die?"

Questions come and doubts the same,
I have no answers to explain;
"Lord, will it ever pass away,
This grief that feels so deep today?"

"Yes, my child, I've heard your plea,
And even though you cannot see;
I'm covering you with my grace,
Upholding you what ere you face.

"Though on Earth 'twas their last breath,
Remember I have conquered death;
Your loved one is home with me,
Secure for all eternity.

"And as you pass from hurt and tears,
To live out your remaining years;
Rejoice! For it soon draws nigh,
That great reunion in the sky."

*"But thanks be to God! He gives us the victory
through our Lord Jesus Christ."
(1 Corinthians 15:57)*

GOD'S GRACE FOR MY LOSS

At times it seems my loss, O Lord,
Is more than I can bear;
Until I humbly bow my heart
And come to you in prayer.

While in the quiet I tell you all
The things that trouble me;
And then I hear you gently speak,
"I see what you can't see.

"The things that hurt you so right now
They're part of my great plan;
I want your heart to find my rest,
Not seek to understand.

"Just simply trust that in my love,
I see beyond today;
And always give my best to those
Who trust me and obey."

As I prepared to leave this place
Where God and I oft meet,
I knew once more His grace had met
My need which was so deep.

Now I can go throughout my day
Content to ere abide;
In Him who fills my emptiness,
While walking by my side.

". . . My grace is sufficient for you, for my power is made perfect in weakness. . . ."
(2 Corinthians 12:9a)

IN OUR LONELINESS

GOD IS OUR FRIEND

FACING LONELINESS

Have you felt the sting of loneliness
And yet you're not alone?
It doesn't matter where you are,
Among a crowd or home.

For somehow you are lost in thoughts
You are not free to share;
And wonder, if you really could,
Would anybody care?

Alone in hurts you've had to bear,
Abuse that's scarred your heart;
While inwardly your soul cries out,
You want a brand-new start.

Well, child, I have good news for you:
There's One who's always there;
He's the Lord of all the lonely,
Who hears and answers prayer.

So lift your wounded heart to Him,
And tell Him how you feel.
He waits for you with open arms,
His love for you is real.

His precious Word will fill your needs;
As He directs the way
To take away your loneliness
And brighten up your days.

". . . Never will I leave you; never will I forsake you. So we can say with confidence, The Lord is my helper; I will not be afraid. What can man do to me?" (Hebrews 13:5b, 6)

LONELINESS

Bible Reading: Mark 15:33–41

Loneliness touches all of us; most have experienced it personally. People can be all around us, yet we feel isolated. Some of us feel lonesome when we cannot share the joy or pain of our experiences. Relationships we thought were secure crumble, leaving us with an emptiness no one can fill. Our hearts cry out, and we are alone. Surely, Jesus encountered the ultimate loneliness while hanging on the Cross. We hear it in His words, *"My God, my God, why have you forsaken me?" (Mark 15:34).*

In this section of devotions, we will look at several aspects of loneliness and discover how the Lord can help us. In preparation, let's think of our Lord saying the following:

My Child, I feel your loneliness, for I have also felt its sting. I know how distant it makes you feel from those around you. I see your tears, the longings of your heart, and your unfulfilled dreams that make all of life seem empty. Come to me. I understand. I love you and wait to hear from you, even when you are sad. I, the Lord God, do not change. I AM is here, and I want to bring my loveliness out of your loneliness. Your Heavenly Father

Prayer: Search out my lonely places, Lord Jesus. I want to live above my loneliness in fellowship with you.

LONELINESS FOR THE APOSTLE PAUL

Bible Reading: 2 Timothy 4:6–22

As we read this passage of Scripture, we discover the apostle Paul was well acquainted with loneliness. Not only was he in prison awaiting a martyr's death, but also he had been forsaken by one who loved this present world more than he did the things of God. Alex, the coppersmith, had done Paul much harm, and at Paul's trial, no human stood with him.

Besides all this, he suffered the discomfort brought on by not having his cloak to keep warm or his books and parchments to help occupy his time. Isn't it amazing that instead of a complaining spirit, Paul exhibits an eternal confidence (vv. 6–8)?

Paul's eternal confidence was in the Lord. He knew he had kept the faith and done his best for God. He was convinced that the things he had done for eternity could not be taken away from him, and one day he would receive the crown of righteousness (v. 8). The loneliness of prison could not change his mind. His eyes were firmly fixed on Jesus.

Are you in a place of loneliness today? Perhaps it's a prison experience, as far as you are concerned. If you are, how will you choose to face it? You can settle for a complaining spirit or determine to lean on Jesus, our eternal confidence. The choice is yours.

Prayer: Guide me into right choices, Lord, even when it's painful.

ETERNAL CONFIDENCE
IN LONELY TIMES

Bible Reading: 2 Timothy 4:6–8; 1 Corinthians 9:24–27

In both of these passages, the writer alludes to the contests at Grecian games. All competitors had to take an oath that they had spent ten months in preparation for the games and that they would not resort to unfair play in the contests. All ran, but only one would receive the prize. The victor was given a wreath made of leaves from the wild olive. Many were willing to undergo strict regulations to contend for this crown—a crown that would soon fade away.

In the Christian life, all who run can obtain a prize. Like the athletes, we need to lay aside anything that hinders us and continue to run the race toward our eternal goal. This includes our emotional baggage, such as loneliness, anxiety, and anger. You may be saying to yourself: How can I do this, considering the loss I'm experiencing? My loneliness is intense, and I'm facing a financial setback as well. The path ahead looks hopeless. I'm in no shape to run a race.

In seasons like these, we need to be open to the ministry of others. Christian friends can help keep us on track, pointing us toward Jesus Christ, our eternal confidence. A listening ear, a loving touch, or a kind deed can bring encouragement and companionship in our lowest moments (Hebrews 4:14–16). As others stand with us, we will find our faith lifting us above our feelings until we can press on toward the goal to win the prize for which God called us. Keep in mind—ours will be an imperishable crown!

Prayer: Father, help me respond to your grace that I might work through my loneliness and continue to run the race for you.

OUR INITIATIVE IN LONELY TIMES

Bible Reading: 2 Timothy 4:9, 11, 13, 21

Fixing our eyes on Jesus in lonely times means more than sitting down and waiting until God moves us. We also have a responsibility to help ourselves—*"faith by itself, if it is not accompanied by action, is dead" (James 2:17).*

The apostle Paul shows his initiative when he writes to Timothy, asking him to come and bring Mark with him *"... because he is helpful to me in my ministry" (v. 11).* Paul may be lonely, but he hasn't given up. He asks for his clock, realizing his body will need it for warmth, and he knows he can make use of his books and parchments.

What can we do to help lift the load of loneliness from our shoulders? Call a friend just to chat, invite someone over, do a kind deed for someone else, treat yourself to a night out, ask for prayer, or seek God.

Suppose you are not lonely. Do you know someone who is? It may be a mother of preschoolers needing to hear an adult voice, a shut-in wanting someone to sit and listen, or your own teenager retreating to his bedroom frequently. Be sensitive and reach out to the lonely, today.

Prayer: Lord Jesus, make your presence real to me in my times of loneliness and use me as an instrument to touch the lonely hearts of others.

THE LORD STANDS WITH US IN LONELY TIMES

Bible Reading: 2 Timothy 4:16–17; Acts 22:30–23:11

Can you sense the loneliness of Paul as he stands before the Sanhedrin? He is surrounded by the leaders of his time, and no one supports him. He used to be one of them, a Pharisee, but even this is of no help to him now. Forsaken by all, he stands alone.

In Acts 23, while shut-up in the barracks, Paul finds one who has not forgotten. His name is Jehovah-shammah, meaning the Lord is there. The Lord comes to His faithful servant with a word of encouragement and direction. *"Take courage! As you have testified about me in Jerusalem, so you must also testify in Rome" (Acts 23:11).*

What do you do when you are faced with what seems like intolerable loneliness, when you feel forsaken by your friends and family, when difficult circumstances seem to hold you back from all human resources, and even God seems far away?

If you are drowning in self-pity, bordering on bitterness, or slipping in and out of depression, listen with your heart to the Word of God for you. *"My Presence will go with you, and I will give you rest" (Exodus 33:14). "A righteous man may have many troubles, but the Lord delivers him from them all" (Psalms 34:19).*

Jehovah-shammah will not desert you in your time of loneliness. The Lord is there!

Prayer: Father, teach me to live above my feelings, that through faith I might rest in your presence.

THE LORD STRENGTHENS US IN LONELY TIMES

Bible Reading: 2 Timothy 4:16–17; 1 Kings 19:1–8

"*At my first defense, no one came to my support, but everyone deserted me. May it not be held against them. But the Lord stood at my side and gave me strength*" *(2 Timothy 4:16, 17b).* We are all acquainted with the exhaustion emotional turmoil can bring. Paul knew it too, but he also realized God's strength could be poured into tired and lonely lives. He experienced it. So did Elijah.

Elijah wasn't in a physical prison, but he certainly felt trapped by circumstances and his own emotions after being used by God to show forth His glory and power. Running from Jezebel, he felt his strength depleted. We find him sitting alone under a broom tree. He had reached his limit of endurance; he wanted to die. Did God forsake him in his hour of need? No, an angel is sent with cake and water telling him, *"Get up and eat, for the journey is too much for you" (1 Kings 19:7).* When he did, he went in the strength of that food for forty days. God tells us in Deuteronomy 33:25b, *". . . your strength will equal your days."*

The same God is available for us today. He sees us where we are. He understands us when we cry out "it is enough." He longs to touch us where we feel weary. He says, *"Come to me, all you who are weary and burdened, and I will give you rest. Take my yoke upon you and learn from me, for I am gentle and humble in heart, and you will find rest for your souls. For my yoke is easy and my burden is light" (Matthew 11:28–30).*

Prayer: My strength is gone, Lord. I'm looking to you to meet my need.

THE LORD USES US IN LONELY TIMES

Bible Reading: 2 Timothy 4:16–17

"But the Lord stood at my side and gave me strength, so that through me the message might be fully proclaimed and all the Gentiles might hear it" (v. 17). This verse bears witness to the presence, power, and purpose of God for His servant, Paul. Today we want to focus on the purpose. Listen to Paul's words while he was in prison at an earlier time in his life. *"Now I want you to know, brothers, that what has happened to me has really served to advance the gospel. As a result, it has become clear throughout the whole palace guard and to everyone else that I am in chains for Christ" (Philippians 1:12, 13).*

Sometimes our circumstances seem like prison. Our loneliness and fears become the chains holding us back from ministry for our Lord. We long to be set free and petition the Lord, telling Him our needs. And as we have been reminded throughout this series of devotions, God's grace never fails us. Perhaps it's time to ask ourselves: are our present circumstances a place of ministry?

Think about what we are told in Hebrews 12:1: *"Therefore, since we are surrounded by such a great cloud of witnesses, let us throw off everything that hinders and the sin that so easily entangles, and let us run with perseverance the race marked out for us."* Let's decide today to lay aside the weight of loneliness and ask God how our prison experience can be used to spread the gospel and glorify His name.

Prayer: Father, redeem my lonely times. Bring ministry out of my misery.

FRIENDS

Lord, I think it's quite a privilege
To have a special friend;
Someone to share my heart with,
And know they'll understand.

In good times of fun and laughter,
Or in life's deepest pain;
A true friend will not desert you,
The bond of love remains.

They will never be offended
When you're honest as can be;
Their listening heart becomes a tool
To heal and set you free.

While we are passing through this life,
We all have need of them,
But let's not just be satisfied
To only have a friend.

For we also should be seeking
To meet another's need;
To comfort and encourage them,
And be a friend, indeed.

We can point the way to Jesus,
Friend closer than a brother;
The One who understands and cares
Far more than any other.

*"A man who has friends must himself be friendly,
But there is a friend who sticks closer than a brother."
(Proverbs 18:24 NKJ)*

THE LORD IN YOUR MIDST

The Lord is mighty in your midst,
And can deliver you;
Just give Him all your loneliness,
And see what He will do.

He'll be your strength in weakness
Give hope instead of fear;
His loving arms will draw you close,
And wipe away your tears.

Your constant friend is who He'll be,
And you'll find others, too;
Who out of His deep love in them,
Will gladly include you.

And as you yield your heart to Him,
Your loneliness will cease;
For with Jesus in the midst of you,
He'll guide you into peace.

"The Lord your God in your midst, the Mighty One, will save; He will rejoice over you with gladness, He will quiet you in His love, He will rejoice over you with singing."
(Zephaniah 3:17 NKJ)

THE HANDS OF GOD

BEHOLD HIS BEAUTY

IN HIS HANDS

When in seasons of great trouble
That I cannot understand,
My heart can still be thankful,
That I'm covered by God's hands.

The mighty hands of God
Are also holding me;
And when my way is dark
His eyes still clearly see.

As He so gently leads me
Into His precious Word;
It's there I find a promise
Like none I've ever heard.

Then as my faith is lifted up,
I rest within His plan;
Assured that He is keeping me
Secure within His hands.

*"For I am the Lord, your God, who takes
hold of your right hand and says to you,
Do not fear; I will help you."
(Isaiah 41:13)*

OUR HANDS—GOD'S HANDS

Bible Reading: Psalms 139:13–18

Our hands are an amazing part of our body. Through them, our touch shows acceptance, gives comfort, and demonstrates affection. We often assist others with our hands, and sometimes we wring them in anxiety. They help us take care of our basic needs as well as help us earn a living. We shake hands in welcome. We write, draw, paint, and type. We fold our hands in prayer and lift them up in praise.

Glance around a room full of people and notice the different kinds of hands—strong hands, tiny hands, loving hands, rough hands, wrinkled hands, crippled hands.

Human hands cause me to think about the hands of God, referred to many times in Scripture. In the following devotions, we will look at some of these passages and discover we are in good hands with God, regardless of what's happening in our lives. To help us focus on God's hands, let's meditate on His Word: *"Yet, O Lord, you are our Father. We are the clay, you are the potter; we are all the work of your hand" (Isaiah 64:8). "For you created my inmost being; you knit me together in my mother's womb. I praise you because I am fearfully and wonderfully made; your works are wonderful, I know that full well" (vv. 13, 14).*

Prayer: I thank you, Father, for the gift of my hands, and that I am the work of your hands.

GOD'S NAIL-SCARRED HANDS

Bible Reading: John 20:24–31

Have you ever thought of yourself as a doubting Thomas? I have. When the other disciples told Thomas they had seen Jesus, he declared: *"Unless I see the nail marks in His hands and put my finger where the nails were, and put my hand into His side, I will not believe it" (v. 20:25).*

Perhaps you are in doubt at this very moment. The decision you must make seems impossible, especially in the light of knowing it may hurt those you love. Your finances are low, and you see no way to pay your bills. You may need humility and courage to talk with someone with whom you disagree, or it could be your health that has you wondering when God is going to show up on your behalf. Did you notice in our Scripture reading that it was Jesus who appeared unexpectedly when the disciples came together one week later? Even locked doors couldn't keep Him away. He wanted Thomas to stop doubting and believe.

No matter how weak our faith is, Jesus wants us to believe that He can work things out. *"Is anything too hard for the Lord?" (Genesis 18:14).* Along with Thomas we can hear Jesus saying, *"Peace be with you!"* When we do, we will exclaim, *"My Lord and my God!"* We can trust the nail-scarred hands of Jesus: nailed to a Cross to bear our sin, revealed to Thomas to enlarge his faith, and inviting us to come just as we are.

Prayer: Thank you, Lord Jesus, for dying for me. Forgive my doubting heart and strengthen my faith in you.

GOD'S HANDS ARE SECURE

Bible Reading: Isaiah 41:8–14

Do your childhood memories include an adult who enjoyed tossing you into the air and catching you? Children usually delight in this attention. Their childlike faith demonstrates how our Heavenly Father wants us to trust Him. His hands will never let us fall. Believe what Deuteronomy 33:27 says, *"The eternal God is your refuge, and underneath are the everlasting arms."*

In today's Bible reading, God assures Israel He is with them in times of fear. Consider Isaiah 41:13: *"For I am the Lord, your God, who takes hold of your right hand and says to you, Do not fear; I will help you."* This verse became a spiritual and emotional stabilizer for me when I faced several surgeries in 1985. Fearful of the unknown, I found even when physically weak, I could trust God and know He was saying to me, *"Fear not."* In Him, I found safety and rest.

Are you facing a difficult circumstance in your life today? Do you fear a decision you need to make? Is insecurity robbing your joy? Our Lord says in Isaiah 41:10, *"Do not fear, for I am with you; do not be dismayed, for I am your God. I will strengthen you and help you; I will uphold you with my righteous right hand."*

Come to Him with childlike faith, and you will find His hands are a place of security.

Prayer: Lord Jesus, I need the security of your hands to enlarge my faith. I want to trust you more.

GOD'S HAND OF DISCIPLINE

Bible Reading: Hebrews 12:1–12

Most of us shy away from discipline and with good reason. It's painful to give out. It's more painful to receive. Yet in our Scripture text, we read, *". . . My son, do not make light of the Lord's discipline, and do not lose heart when He rebukes you, because the Lord disciplines those He loves"* (v. 5).

Thinking about how we discipline our own children (in love) can help us understand God's desire to correct us. We discipline our children to protect them from harm. We want them to develop responsible behavior and to realize the consequences of having their own way. Even when our children are grown, we sometimes face tough situations concerning decisions they are making. Take, for instance, couples living together before marriage, which our culture accepts today. As Christians, we need to stand firm on God's Word. Our standards may seem difficult to our children, but God's truth will not allow us to do otherwise.

"Our fathers disciplined us for a little while as they thought best; but God disciplines us for our good, that we may share in His holiness" (v. 10). Our heavenly Father knows when we need correction. He desires for us to mature in every area of our lives. Our loving Father wants us to forsake sin. He yearns for a deeper relationship with us. He, alone, knows just the amount of pressure it will take to accomplish His work in us. For the Lord to withhold His hand of discipline would be to withhold His love.

Prayer: Father God, teach me not to struggle against your loving hand of discipline, but to surrender my will to yours.

OUR TIMES ARE IN GOD'S HANDS

Bible Reading: Psalms 31

We easily accept that our times are in God's hands when everything is going well. But how do we react when we feel hemmed in on all sides? What will we do if we become a victim of evil through no fault of our own? Many face losing a job after years of faithful service. Some are crippled in an accident that wasn't their fault, etc. Can we trust God's hands in the perplexing and desperate times of life?

David did, and in our Bible reading he sets an example as he seeks refuge from his enemies. He calls out, *"Free me from the trap that is set for me, for you are my refuge. Into your hands I commit my spirit; redeem me, O Lord, the God of truth . . . I trust in you, O Lord; I say 'you are my God.' My times are in your hands; deliver me from my enemies and from those who pursue me"* (vv. 4, 5; 14, 15).

In 1 Thessalonians 3:2, 3, the apostle Paul sends Timothy to strengthen and encourage the church so no one would be unsettled by the trials Paul and Timothy were going through. He adds, *"You know quite well we were destined for them."*

Difficult seasons of life may surprise us, but they don't surprise our Sovereign God. He invites us to say with David, *"My times are in your hands, O Lord."* He is El Shaddai—the all-sufficient one. He knows every dilemma we face and is abundantly available in tight places.

Prayer: Father, I surrender my times into your hands. You are the potter; I am the clay. Come to me now as I wait in your presence.

GOD'S VICTORIOUS HAND

Bible Reading: Psalms 118

The psalmist describes a time he was surrounded on every side by nations who wanted to harm him. He says he was pushed back and about to fall. This reminds me of the apostle Paul, who found himself in a besetting storm while on his way to Rome. In Acts 27:22, he speaks words of victory while the storm is raging: *"But now I urge you to keep up your courage, because not one of you will be lost; only the ship will be destroyed."*

Sometimes, while listening to others share, I wonder how they handle their personal battles. One of my friends has prayed 43 years for her husband to become a Christian, but he has not. She is surrounded often by difficult behavior. This constant load of stress has broken her physically and emotionally at times, but never spiritually. She always comes out of the battle standing up because, like David, she believes the Word of God and proclaims with him: *"The Lord is my strength and my song; he has become my salvation. Shouts of joy and victory resound in the tents of the righteous: 'The Lord's right hand has done mighty things!'" (Psalms 118:14, 15).*

Are you or someone you know under attack on all sides? Does victory seem impossible? Take a look at the life of Jehoshaphat in 2 Chronicles 20. Listen to the instructions he gives his people in verse 15: *"Do not be afraid or discouraged because of this vast army. For the battle is not yours, but God's."*

Prayer: Father, I am confused and my path is dark. Teach me to live in victory— to rest in knowing the battle is yours.

OUR LIVES IN GOD'S HANDS

Bible Reading: 1 Corinthians 9:24–27

Have you heard words like these lately? "Do you want to reduce the risk of heart attack and stroke? Begin today by lowering your intake of fat and cholesterol." "Exercising three times a week will give you more energy and increase your life span." At times, it seems as if we are bombarded by reports on how to feel younger, become healthier, and live a better quality of life for a longer time. I agree that eating properly and exercising regularly are good things. I'm doing it for my own heart condition. But let's not lose sight of 1 Timothy 4:8: *"For physical training is of some value, but godliness has value for all things, holding promise for both the present life and the life to come."*

In our Bible reading, we learn that winning life's race has little to do with things that are temporary, but everything to do with receiving a crown that will last forever. In the book of James we are reminded not to boast about tomorrow as our life is only *". . . a mist that appears for a little while and then vanishes" (James 4:14).* Job, in his distress, expresses himself in this manner: *"Man's days are determined; you have decreed the number of his months and have set limits he cannot exceed" (Job 14:5).*

As we take care of our physical bodies, let's not neglect to nurture our spirit, as it needs to be fed and exercised daily as well. It will help us win the race. Listen to what God says in Proverbs 3:1–2: *"My son, do not forget my teaching, but keep my commands in your heart, for they will prolong your life many years."* Our lives are in God's hands!

Prayer: Thank you, Lord, that you know the number of my days. Teach me to live with eternity in view.

GOD'S COMFORT TO OUR SOUL

God holds us up and soothes our hurts.
His tender touch dries our tears.
He binds the wounds of broken hearts,
His gentle whisper quiets our fears.

God understands our fragile emotions;
His unfailing love embraces our frame.
He lifts us up when we can't go on,
His powerful Word is ours to claim.

God's peaceful presence eases our pain,
His skillful hands are in control;
He assures our hearts we're safe in Him,
He sends us comfort to delight our soul.

*"In the multitude of my anxieties within me,
your comforts delight my soul."
(Psalms 94:19 NKJ)*

LOVING-KINDNESS

Come—find my loving-kindness, child,
Walk within my plan;
It's time to lay your struggle down,
And rest within my hands.

I know it seems it can't be true,
The way you feel inside;
But conflicts fade within my love
It's safe in me to hide.

I've walked this painful path with you,
And bottled up each tear;
I understand your deepest thoughts—
The reasons for your fear.

My love will never punish you;
I could not—can't you see?
For everything that you deserved
I bore at Calvary.

Your conflicts and emotional pain
Are not too much for me;
Yes, even from obsessive thoughts,
My love can set you free.

So focus now upon my love,
Unfailing it will be;
For with cords of loving-kindness,
I've bound you unto me.

"See I have inscribed you on the palms of my hands; your walls are continually before me."
(Isaiah 49:16)

IN TROUBLED TIMES

HE REFRESHES OUR SOUL

TROUBLES TURN TO REST

Trouble abounded on every side,
I knew not what to do;
I came to seek my Lord in prayer,
As He would have me to.

With my eyes focused on the Lord,
He said, "Now don't you fear;
Just take up your position,
Stand firm, for I am near.

"The battle is not yours, you know,
It all belongs to me;
And I'll be with you all the way
So wait for me and see."

As I bowed my head to worship Him
And praise His Holy Name;
Faith rose up inside of me,
His Word was mine to claim.

While waiting for my Lord to work,
A song He placed within;
He drew me close—assuring me,
This battle He would win.

And now there's rest on every side,
Anxieties have ceased;
For my Lord who fights the battle
Has brought me into peace.

". . . 'Do not be afraid nor dismayed because of this great multitude, for the battle is not yours, but God's.' "
(2 Chronicles 20:15b NKJ)

TROUBLE ON EVERY SIDE

Bible Reading: 2 Chronicles 1–4; Matthew 11:28–30

How does King Jehoshaphat respond when he is rebuked for his alliance with the wicked King Ahab? He responds by repenting, going throughout his kingdom to bring the people back to the Lord, and appointing judges in the land (2 Chronicles 19). Soon after reinforcing the Lord's commands, Jehoshaphat receives bad news: *"A vast army is coming against you from Edom" (2 Chronicles 20:2a).* Jehoshaphat is alarmed! Trouble surrounds him on every side.

Perhaps adverse circumstances are erupting in your life today. I recall the day I discovered my daughter and her husband were having marital problems. Two months later, I learned the same was true for my son's family. Believe me, I was alarmed! But this was only the beginning. The situation escalated into false accusations, threats of violence, divorce, and much more. I faced troubles on all sides. My heart was broken. But King Jehoshaphat's response to trouble showed me the way through these difficulties.

The first thing Jehoshaphat did after receiving the bad news was to inquire of the Lord and proclaim a fast. All of Judah came together to seek help from the Lord. When we are in trouble, there is no better place to begin. Whatever our trials, Jesus says, *"Come to me, all you who are weary and burdened, and I will give you rest" (Matthew 11:28).*

Let's examine our own lives with some searching questions: Am I seeking God in the midst of my troubles? Have I invited His wisdom into my circumstances? Will I trust Him to do what's best for all concerned?

Prayer: Lord Jesus, help me lay my troubles at your feet.

SEEKING GOD IN TROUBLED TIMES

Bible Reading: 2 Chronicles 20:5–12

King Jehoshaphat's prayer models for us three ways to seek God in troubled times. First, he acknowledged that God rules over all. Power and might are in God's hands—no one can withstand Him (vv. 6, 7). Do we praise God for who He is in the midst of our difficulties? Jeremiah 32:17 can encourage us in times like these: *"Ah, Sovereign Lord, you made the heavens and the earth by your great power and outstretched arm. Nothing is too hard for you."*

Next, Jehoshaphat remembers God's faithfulness to the Jews in times past. *"If calamity comes upon us . . . we will stand in your presence before the temple that bears your Name and will cry out to you in our distress and you will hear us and save us"* (v. 9).

When we recall God's faithfulness, our confidence builds and we can release ourselves and our problems to God. We gain the courage to lean on His promises. *"The righteous cry out, and the Lord hears them; He delivers them from all their troubles. The Lord is close to the broken-hearted and saves those who are crushed in spirit. A righteous man may have many troubles, but the Lord delivers him from them all"* (Psalms 34:17–19).

Lastly, Jehoshaphat humbly admits, *". . . We do not know what to do, but our eyes are upon you"* (2 Chronicles 20:12). Oh, that our trials would lead us to seek God in humility—with hope.

Prayer: Father, I acknowledge your sovereignty. I thank you for your faithfulness. Hear my cry for help! I am weak and lack direction, but I will not lose hope because my eyes are upon you.

DO NOT BE AFRAID

Bible Reading: 2 Chronicles 20:13–15

As the men, women, and children of Judah stood before the Lord, the Spirit of the Lord came upon Jahaziel giving him directions for battle. *". . . This is what the Lord says to you: 'Do not be afraid or discouraged because of this vast army. For the battle is not yours, but God's'" (v. 15).*

The battles we face in life often involve relationships, and if we aren't listening to the Holy Spirit, these conflicts can stir up trouble and hurt innocent people. Sometimes it's conflict that arises over change in the church. We confront others because we want our own way. We face inner struggles when we need to ask a brother or sister in Christ for forgiveness.

Years ago in a revival meeting, the Holy Spirit asked me to go to an individual and attempt to resolve our differences. I was afraid, but God gave me the courage to go. Imagine my discouragement when the person refused to talk with me. I was comforted by the evangelist, who explained to me that I had done all I could do. The battle was not mine but God's. A number of years later the individual contacted me, and the circle of forgiveness was complete.

Just as the Holy Spirit spoke to the people of Judah, He speaks to us. You do not need to be afraid or discouraged when struggles arise, within or without, for He is with you. *"Never will I leave you; never will I forsake you. So we say with confidence, 'The Lord is my helper; I will not be afraid. What can man do to me?'" (Hebrews 13:5, 6).*

Prayer: Indwelling Spirit, please give me courage to face my fears and overcome them through you.

TAKE UP YOUR POSITION

Bible Reading: 2 Chronicles 20:16, 17

Now that the Lord has declared He is fighting this battle, Jehoshaphat and the people of Judah are told to take up their positions and stand firm. As believers, our position is in Christ. *"Therefore, since we have been justified through faith, we have peace with God through our Lord Jesus Christ, through whom we have gained access by faith into this grace in which we now stand" (Romans 5:1, 2).* God's grace in which we stand will be sufficient for every battle we face. 2 Corinthians 12:9a says: *"My grace is sufficient for you, for my power is made perfect in weakness."*

But some might ask, "How can I be in Christ?" I tell the children I work with that it's as easy as ABC: A. <u>Admit</u> that you are a sinner in need of forgiveness. *"For all have sinned and fall short of the glory of God" (Romans 3:23).* B. <u>Believe</u> in the Lord Jesus. C. <u>Confess</u> with your mouth Jesus is Lord. *"If you confess with your mouth, 'Jesus is Lord,' and believe in your heart that God raised Him from the dead, you will be saved. For it is with your heart that you believe and are justified, and it is with your mouth that you confess and are saved" (Romans 10:9, 10).*

For those of us who are in Christ, let's take up our position, and face our enemy with confidence in Jesus and His Word. If you aren't sure of your place in Christ, why not open your heart to Him today?

Prayer: Thank you, Father, that I am safe in you. I can trust you, even as the battle rages.

STAND FIRM

*Bible Reading: 2 Chronicles 20:16, 17;
Ephesians 6:10–18*

What does it mean for a Christian to stand firm in life's battles? While thinking on this question, I was reminded of the small three-tier stand I have in my bathroom. It has one wobbly leg that can be a problem. In order for it to support the items I keep on it, it must be fastened together in just the right way. Its foundation must be secure. Likewise, we can only stand firm when our foundation is in Christ. 1 Corinthians 3:11 tells us: *"For no one can lay any foundation other than the one already laid, which is Jesus Christ."*

As believers, we are also told, *"Put on the full armor of God so that you can take your stand against the devil's schemes" (Ephesians 6:11).* God's armor helps us stand firm against our enemy. We need to be covered completely because our enemy delights to pounce on us when we are in trouble. He knows our weakest point and aims for it. But when we're clothed with God's armor, it will protect us in every battle.

Jehoshaphat provides an amazing example for us. He didn't give up in his day of trouble, but chose to stand firm and follow God's directions. He and his people were ready for their final instructions. *"Go out to face them tomorrow, and the Lord will be with you" (2 Chronicles 20:17).* Whatever the challenge of our tomorrow, let's determine to stand firm—assured the Lord is with us.

Prayer: All Sufficient One, give me the strength to stand firm in the challenges of life—confident you are with me.

PRAISE AND FAITH

*Bible Reading: 2 Chronicles 20:18–21;
Ephesians 4:25–32*

After King Jehoshaphat and the people of Judah and Jerusalem received the Word of the Lord, they fell down and worshiped Him. Some of the Levites stood up and praised God loudly. The next morning King Jehoshaphat prepared the people to face their enemies by instructing them to have faith in God and His prophets. He reminded them that their faith in the Lord and His Word would uphold them and bring them success. He appointed men to go ahead of the army singing and praising God.

Today's Scripture brings to mind a situation I faced recently involving family members. I was seeking God about the problem, but I still had a mix of feelings the day I received an invitation to their home. I accepted it, while dreading to confront the issue at hand. I felt like I would be "walking on eggs" in their presence. In the meantime, the Lord spoke to me concerning the matter. I was to line up my life with Ephesians 4:25–32.

As I submitted to the Word of the Lord, praise and faith began to rise up inside of me just as it had in Jehoshaphat and his people. I bowed my heart and worshiped. My faith was strengthened. My heavy spirit was replaced by a song.

How about you? Are you ready to respond to God's Word concerning your battle? He'll build up your faith and put a song in your heart. It could be a step toward victory. It was for Jehoshaphat—it was for me.

Prayer: Faithful Father, open my heart to your Word. Lead me in the way of praise and faith. I want to live in victory.

REST ON EVERY SIDE

Bible Reading: 2 Chronicles 20:22–30

I have always been amazed that Jehoshaphat appointed singers to go before the army, praising God. It speaks to me of the power found in praise. When we rise to meet our day with a song in our heart—even when we don't feel like it—the light of Jesus shines forth. I recall a friend of mine who was scolded by others for praising God in the midst of her trials. These dear ones seemed to have no concept of the inner joy of a Christian, who stands firm in Christ and leaves the battle to Him.

Notice what happens as Jehoshaphat moves by faith and appoints singers to go before the army praising God. The Lord ambushes their enemies, and the army of Jehoshaphat is victorious. Jehoshaphat and his people, who not so long ago were crying out to God in desperation, have found the victory. With their eyes upon God, God led the way. *"And the kingdom of Jehoshaphat was at peace, for his God had given him rest on every side" (v. 30).*

God desires peace for each of us, regardless of our troubles. He invites us to seek Him. He will quiet our fears as we stand firm, believing His Word. He delights to hear our praises as we walk by faith, even when the way is not clear. He longs to bring us, as He did Jehoshaphat, into rest on every side. Will we let Him?

Prayer: Wonderful Lord, teach me to walk in your ways, with my eyes upon you. Lead me into peace and rest on every side.

WHEN TROUBLES COME

When troubles come, as we know they will,
God has a special plan;
And though the way is dark for us,
There's rest within His hand.

It may be illness that has come,
So swiftly to disrupt;
And bring into our life new change,
Through things we must give up.

A loved one may have gone ahead
We taste of lonely days;
While silently some would wish
They, too, could go away.

We're not as strong—we must slow down,
In much of what we do;
And money is in its final stretch,
It seems for quite a few.

Yet no matter what our troubles
Our God extends His hand;
We cannot go where He is not,
While living in His plan.

He wants to give us all we need,
So let's just stop to pray,
And lay our troubles at His feet,
So He can guide our way.

"God is our refuge and strength,
A very present help in trouble."
(Psalms 46:1 NKJ)

VICTORY IN THE STORM

Keep my eyes upon you, Jesus,
Or I'll not make it through;
Don't let me think "what might have been"
Nor even what I'll do.

Just let me rest in who you are:
My guide both true and bright,
Companion in the valley deep,
My candle in the night.

And let me trust because you say
Before your sheep you go;
You've walked the path I now must take
It's every step you know.

You understand why life has turned
And brought me to this place;
You are my shield—protecting me
As storm winds 'round me race.

My coming in and going out,
Both are preserved by you;
And in your presence I find peace
No matter what I do.

I cannot change my circumstances,
The way that things will be;
But I am standing on your Word
You are my victory!

"Yet in all these things we are more than conquerors through Him who loved us."
(Romans 8:37 NKJ)

HOW CAN I KNOW HIM?

1. REMEMBER GOD LOVES YOU: "For God so loved the world that He gave His one and only Son, that whoever believes in Him shall not perish but have eternal life" (John 3:16).

2. RECOGNIZE YOU ARE A SINNER: "For all have sinned and fall short of the glory of God" (Romans 3:23).

3. REALIZE YOU WILL RECEIVE EITHER THE WAGES OF SIN OR THE GIFT OF GOD: "For the wages of sin is death, but the gift of God is eternal life in Christ Jesus our Lord" (Romans 6:23).

4. REFLECT ON GOD'S PENALTY FOR SIN: "God made Him who had no sin to be sin for us, so that in Him we might become the righteousness of God" (2 Corinthians 5:21).

5. REPENT OF YOUR SINS AND TURN FROM THEM: "In the past God overlooked such ignorance, but now commands all people everywhere to repent" (Acts 17:30).

6. RECEIVE THE GIFT OF GOD BY INVITING JESUS INTO YOUR LIFE AND BELIEVING ON HIS NAME: "Yet to all who received Him, to those who believed in His name, He gave the right to become children of God" (John 1:12).

PRAYER: Lord Jesus, I know I am a sinner. Forgive me of all my sins. Thank you for dying on the Cross and taking my punishment. I believe you are the Son of God who died, was buried, and the third day arose from the dead. Come into my life and be my Savior. Teach me how to live for you. In Jesus' Name, Amen.

ASSURANCE

"I tell you the truth; he who believes has everlasting life" (John 6:47). "I write these things to you who believe in the name of the Son of God so that you may know that you have eternal life" (1 John 5:13).